Andreas Glombitza

Transgression in Cyril Tourneur's "A revenger's tragedy" - an analysis according to George Bataille

65668

GRIN - Verlag für akademische Texte

Der GRIN Verlag mit Sitz in München hat sich seit der Gründung im Jahr 1998 auf die Veröffentlichung akademischer Texte spezialisiert. Die Verlagswebseite www.grin.com ist für Studenten, Hochschullehrer und andere Akademiker die ideale Plattform, ihre Fachtexte, Studienarbeiten, Abschlussarbeiten oder Dissertationen einem breiten Publikum zu präsentieren.

Dokument Nr. V33533 aus dem GRIN Verlagsprogramm

Andreas Glombitza

Transgression in Cyril Tourneur's "A revenger's tragedy" - an analysis according to George Bataille

GRIN Verlag

Bibliografische Information der Deutschen Nationalbibliothek: Die Deutsche Bibliothek
verzeichnet diese Publikation in der Deutschen Nationalbibliografie; detaillierte bibliografische Daten sind im Internet über http://dnb.d-nb.de/ abrufbar.

1. Auflage 2004
Copyright © 2004 GRIN Verlag
http://www.grin.com/
Druck und Bindung: Books on Demand GmbH, Norderstedt Germany
ISBN 978-3-638-77224-2

Eberhard-Karls Universität Tübingen
Seminar für Englische Philologie
PS II: The Ethics of Reading

WS 2003/04

Transgression in Cyril Tourneur's
A Revenger's Tragedy: an analysis according to George Bataille.

Andreas Glombitza

Magister: Rhetorik/
Englische Linguistik
Fachsemester 05
20. 04. 2004

Contents:

1. Introduction

Vindice, the protagonist of *A Revenger's Tragedy*, is not easy to judge. When it comes to the question whether to condemn, applaud or pity him, we are caught within conflicting emotions. Undoubtedly, he and his brother commit acts of horrible violence – they nail down the dukes tongue with a dagger, force him to see his wife commit adultery with his own 'bastard son' and finally kill him. But nevertheless, and not without an uncanny after-taste, Vindice also inspires our sympathy.

The surrealist philosopher Georges Bataille has, within the frame of his integral work on life itself, worked out a theory of the social function of taboos and the necessity of their very definition by transgression. It is a concept of temporary permeability of inviolable borders which could provide an interesting and helpful framework for a closer examination of Vindice's behaviour and its results.

After getting familiar with some of Bataille's most basic concepts and particular features of his thought, we will try to determine the role Bataille attributes to the concept of taboo and transgression within society. A brief look at Michel Foucault's discussion of this concept will complement to this. After having considered some complications concerning the Christian tradition, we should be able to concern ourselves with an according analysis of the play. A few introductory observations about plot, protagonist and underlying ideas will be necessary until we can finally try to employ the concept of transgression as our guide through the labyrinth of revenge.

2. Analysis

2.1 An outline of George Bataille's theory of transgression

If there is a centre of gravity around which George Bataille's work revolves, it is certainly the paradox. All of his observations seem to somehow stem from and end in paradoxical propositions that are necessarily never fully graspable by reason. Life as such, for Bataille, grounds on a principle of paradox; on the irreconcilable, but still interconnected and interdependent fields of life and its proliferation and the discontinuity of individual death – the line of intersection being in the violence of eroticism. "For

Bataille, human experience is an experience of limits and these limits are defined by the fact that the condition of life for human beings is the recognition of death"[1]. We always have to bear in mind that his theories are not meant to be completely 'understood' in a traditional sense. Knowledge itself, in his frame, is a highly elusive and paradoxical thing: the more we know, he argues, the more knowledge tends to slip through our fingers, creating slippage itself in its accumulation. "[…] [Bataille] believed that a genuine knowledge needed to recognise its own essential incompleteness and the fact that it had to be completed through the embrace of a complementary 'non-knowledge' [...]"[2] – "truth", for him, therefore, "lay not so much in knowledge itself, but in the margin between knowledge and non-knowledge"[3] [4]. Pairs like this "knowledge and non-knowledge", which would at first glance seem binary, can be found everywhere in his works. But we have to be careful – neither is a mechanism of Hegelian dialectics at work here nor do we have simple dualisms (or binarities, or complementarities, or antagonisms)[5]. A concept similar to, but not the same as dialectics – a relationship between a positive and element of some 'entirely other', which is still in some miraculous contact with this positive, though not in the sense of an antithesis and without a following "Aufhebung" - will be crucial for our observations.

When it comes to the relationship of the individual to the collective, to what we may call society, Bataille's attitude is quite radical: the individual as such, separated from all social relations, is non-existent.

> It is impossible to conceive of individuals other than as social beings and thus as being separable from the society of which they are an integral part. […] At the heart of the social lies the convergence of work and sexuality and this convergence is intimately linked to our understanding of death.[6]

While for him "[…] social relations are the fundamental element of human existence [...]"[7], Bataille also examines what he calls the 'inner experience. Pursuing his claim for integrity, he thought that it made "[…] no sense to analyse social relations independently of the inner subjectivity of the individuals comprised within a given social

---

[1] Richardson, Michael. Georges Bataille p. 98
[2] Richardson, Michael. Georges Bataille p. 40
[3] Richardson, Michael. Georges Bataille p. viii
[4] the way Richardson puts it somewhat poetically – "[...] knowledge needs to be recognised as what it is: a momentary gleam in the night that fades in the moment it is born" – reveals striking resemblance to Arthur Koestler's concept of 'bisociation' ('dual association'; two mental 'operative fields' momentarily intersecting;) which seems to be of a similar nature and is, according to Koestler, the "characteristic feature of any original creative process, whether in art or in discovery";
[5] cp. Gasché, Rodolphe. The Heterological Almanac p. 159
[6] Richardson, Michael. Georges Bataille p. 98
[7] Richardson, Michael. Georges Bataille p. 97

3

network" and thus wanted to cover "[...] both the internal and external aspects of social being."[8]

2.1.1 The taboo and its social significance

To give an idea of the nature of the taboo Bataille reminds us of the fifth commandment, "thou shalt not kill", the recitation of which usually accompanies the blessings of the armies before going to war. Quite an odd practice, it would seem: more or less immediately afterwards the soldiers are of course allowed and expected to kill and, accordingly, to transgress. The ceremony nonetheless carries all thinkable features of earnestness and the air of solemnity, but obviously it does not in any way hinder any soldier from doing his bloody duties. The clue Bataille provides to solve this riddle focuses on the specific nature of the common killing taboo (which is underlying for the fifth commandment and, for Bataille, the distinctive feature of every human society): were the interdict of killing under the command of reason, as we would assume, the soldiers would, logically concluding, have two possibilities: To take the interdict as absolute and obey by not killing anyone – or to fight and take the taboo as deceitful. Both rational alternatives would, serving as basis for a decision, mark a concerned person as at least unsuitable for being a soldier. But, Bataille explains, although the reasonable world is built on taboos, the taboos themselves are not necessarily reasonable[9]. According to his argumentation, the origin of the killing taboo probably falls in one with the origin of war[10]: in a (somewhat hypothetical) primeval effort to tame violence – "um die beiden Welten zu scheiden"[11] - it would not have sufficed to pose a calm and reasonable opposition against it: the 'opposition' had to exert violence itself, at the same time employing the exertion with an intense negative emotional charge and thus marking violence as false. Reason alone wouldn't have had enough authority to overcome it, to define the point of transition[12], only the elementary emotions of fright and deterrence could resist in the aspect of excessive rage.

[8] Richardson, Michael. Georges Bataille p. 97
[9] cp. Bataille, Georges. Der heilige Eros p. 59
[10] cp. Bataille, Georges. Der heilige Eros p. 60
[11] Bataille, Georges. Der heilige Eros p. 59
[12] cp. Bataille, Georges. Der heilige Eros p. 59

This is characteristic of the nature of the taboo: while it enables a world of relative stability, of reason and peace, it is in itself something like a shiver, striking not reason, but the heart, the emotional in us"[13].

Thus, the social significance of the taboo could be described as following: For society, interdicts or taboos – the manifestations of authority - have the function of marking off threatening occurrences, persons or things and inhibit violent acts. They enable us to maintain our reasonable everyday-life world – by granting a crucial condition which we can technically term "homogeneity". Only on the basis of an artificial, hypothetical (and in fact somewhat treacherous) homogeneity we are able to compare things that would be otherwise incomparable; we can connect, for instance, one tree to another only by virtue of counting both to the same category 'tree'. But at a closer look, the two 'trees' have things in common only with respect to other certain categories – they won't, speaking in absolute terms, be in any way identical[14]. We make up a more or less precise definition of what may still be called a tree and what not. To be able to trace the differences between two elements of a category, we always have to stay on some safe ground by ignoring other differences – taking them all into account would reveal nothing than chaos. It is this artificial construct of homogeneity that transmutates the outer world from a cold, odd and incomprehensible place into our supposedly predictable and secure inner home, and it does so by denying and excluding everything that looks odd and incomprehensible. "Homogeneity signifies commensurability of elements and consciousness of this commensurability"[15]. With due brevity, homogeneity enables us to categorize the world around us – the best symbol for it being money, which allows us to compare elements and even services by assigning them a value. Thus it becomes the basis of the world of work. For Bataille, taboos are the pillars of this homogeneity and at the same time something like a watershed within our world – constituting the borderline to something "entirely other", something driven to - and yet coming from - the outside. This outside is the realm of the heterogeneous. It is constituted by all that had to be denied in order to establish homogeneity. But, as it seems, we can neither live with nor without this heterogeneous: by its incessant intrusion into the homogeneous world from outside, it constitutes a 'static equilibrium'. Such push-ins of

---

[13] cp. Bataille, Georges. Der heilige Eros p. 59
[14] we just have to think of how many instances of entirely different 'trees' may cross our paths – the giant redwoods in a national park, the figures drawn by linguists to explore sentence structure ('tree-diagrams'), all the cables in a car taken together ('Kabelbaum' in German) – they all legitimately bear the name 'tree' by virtue of a loose connection to some generally agreed concept;
[15] cited after Gasché, Rodolphe. The Heterological Almanac p. 159

the heterogeneous, for example, occur through mediation by the executive powers that are in touch with its sphere, our kings or leaders;[16] that particular instance is termed "imperial heterogeneity"[17] by Gasché. He argues that the field[18] of the heterogeneous is in fact polarized and divided between "high" and "low".

> The heterogeneous realm is deeply polarized by the distinction between high and low. […] [T]o the low is attributed all that arises from excrement, from the miserable, from night; to the high everything aligned with the serene, the pure, the sun, etc. If the homogenous part of society requires an opening towards heterogeneous elements, this means that it addresses itself to the high, to the sublime, to find its orient and its orientation there.[19]

It is important to note that the 'heterogeneous' is in fact not merely 'other' in the sense of the Greek word; the word commonly denotes something opposite or different to something else, and therefore something already largely defined by being the negative of something given – but here it means rather 'otherness' itself[20] [21]. "[…] [H]omogeneity […] does not embrace all of society, but only one of its parts (and thus is already limited by an exterior), functioning necessarily through the exclusion and the rejection of an unuseful part […]", as Gasché puts it. The homogeneity of society, an artificial construct on the frail foundations of reason, a world were things can be stuffed into neat categories[22], the prerequisite of our social fabric, is under permanent threat and requires "[…] an authority foreign to the homogenous […]"[23].

Where "high" or imperative heterogeneous elements are in contact with the homogeneous world, accordingly, we can find the agents of authority: "The heterogeneous to which the homogeneous world has recourse is of an imperative and sovereign nature".

---

[16] cf. Gasché, Rodolphe. *The Heterological Almanac* p. 166
[17] accordingly, primitive cultures commonly attributed divine powers to their chieftains;
[18] the struggle for fitting terms already points to the ultimate hopelessness of the attempt of grasping by reason what is by nature everything that reason excludes – it is of course neither a field, nor a sphere, nor has it any similarity to any geometrical body – perhaps in some sense it is „what is not ‚kosmos'" - ‚chaos' then;
[19] Gasché, Rodolphe. *The Heterological Almanac* p. 165
[20] cf. Gasché, Rodolphe. *The Heterological Almanac* p. 158
[21] this leads Gasché to the odd-sounding proposition that "[a]s a site for the play of differences, the heterogeneous inscribes within itself the difference between itself and its opposite" (Gasché, Rodolphe. *The Heterological Almanac* p. 164)
[22] science and scientific method – including Batailles own methods - are even more essentially dependent on the comparability of elements and therefore homogeneity; science has a 'zero tolerance' towards the heterogeneous; therefore, the attempt of analysing the heterogeneous from within the core of homogeneity remains a questionable effort; cp. Gasché, Rodolphe. *The Heterological Almanac* p. 196
[23] Gasché, Rodolphe. *The Heterological Almanac* p. 161

> [...] [I]n homogenous society the function of safeguarding static equilibrium is incumbent on the state. The state, however, is still a part of the structure of social homogeneity. It is not, in an immediate way, the authority of the heterogenous in the homogenous world. It constitutes rather an intermediary formation between homogenous structure and the heterogeneous elements indispensable to the maintenance of order.[24]

This inherently *irrational* character of the taboo and the authorities concerned with its maintenance, the fact that they draw their power from something that is beyond these boundaries of our common everyday-life world, must always be taken into account.

Thus, shaking our idea of what the word 'taboo' implies, Bataille claims that the occasional violation of an inviolable taboo doesn't mean it has ceased to be inviolable - and even, to point out the apparent absurdity: "The taboo exists only to be broken".[25] This is the reason why the killing taboo, though valid in general, has never stood in the way of any war. In fact, the contrary is the case, as Bataille continues: without the taboo, war itself would have been impossible. In the kingdom of animals, there is no taboo at all – accordingly, animals have no wars. Their violence is, above the plane of raw fighting, unorganised. War, on the other hand, is nothing else than organised violence, transgression of the killing taboo. This act of transgression is not at all the same as the unorganised violence that occurs among animals: it is violence of a different quality, exerted by a reasonable creature temporarily putting reason into its duty.[26] The taboo constitutes the threshold beyond which such violence becomes temporarily permissible - *war* means that the collective has gone beyond that threshold; it is in nature totally different from violence ignorant of the taboo. Only without its limited character, it would be the return to bestial violence.

> The imposition of the taboo implied at the same time the need to transgress it, the provision of which primitive society made within a ritual form that allowed, at specific times and occasions, free play [...]. This was the time that the world would be 'turned upside down' and all that had to be denied in the cause of the principle of work was brought back into the social sphere. Transgression was thus an essential component of the taboo. It did not stand outside it, nor was the impulse behind transgression to subvert the taboo but on the contrary to ensure its effectiveness.[27]

---

[24] Gasché, Rodolphe. *The Heterological Almanac* p. 164f
[25] cf. Bataille, Georges. Der heilige Eros p. 59
[26] cf. Bataille, Georges. Der heilige Eros p. 60
[27] Richardson, Michael. Georges Bataille p. 102

Transgression should thus "[...] not be confused with a sense of disorder: it obeyed its own rules (which were often more rigorous than those of the taboo) and implied the consciousness, not the absence, of limits."[28] Accordingly, transgression is at one with the taboo itself, they are two sides of one coin, constituting defining agents of social life – transgression does not spoil the taboo's constancy.

2.1.2 Measuring a thin line: Michel Foucault's *A Preface to Transgression*

In his essay *A Preface to Transgression* Michel Foucault gives a detailed picture of the implications of the phenomenon and the peculiar relationship between limit and transgression. According to Foucault, "[t]ransgression is an action that involves the limit, that narrow zone of a line where it displays the flash of its passage, but perhaps also its entire trajectory, even its origin; it is likely that transgression has its entire space in the line it crosses"[29].

The border and the act of its transgression owe each other their existence: a border that could not be crossed would be non-existent; transgression, that wouldn't seriously cross a border, would be mere fancy[30].

He concludes that "[t]ransgression, then, is not related to the limit as black to white, the prohibited to the lawful, [and] the outside to the inside [...]"[31]. It his inherent to it, 'carved into it', and cannot be removed.

Transgression "[...] serves as a glorification of what it excludes: the limit opens violently onto the limitless, finds itself suddenly carried away by the content it had rejected and fulfilled by this alien plenitude that invades it to the core of its being". Foucault demands that transgression must be "detached from its questionable associations to ethics if we want to understand it and to begin thinking from it in the space it denotes; it must be liberated form the scandalous or subversive [...]"[32]. Transgression, in fact, had nothing to do with subversion:

---

[28] Richardson, Michael. Georges Bataille p. 102
[29] Faubion, James, Ed. Aesthetics, Method, and Epistemology: Essential Works of Foucault p. 73
[30] cp. Faubion, James, Ed. Aesthetics, Method, and Epistemology: Essential Works of Foucault p. 73
[31] Faubion, James, Ed. Aesthetics, Method, and Epistemology: Essential Works of Foucault p. 73f
[32] Faubion, James, Ed. Aesthetics, Method, and Epistemology: Essential Works of Foucault p. 74

> Transgression doesn't seek to oppose one thing to another, nor does it achieve its purpose through mockery or by upsetting the solidity of foundations; Transgression contains nothing negative, but affirms limited being – affirms the limitless into which it leaps as it opens this zone to existence for the first time.[33]

On the other hand, this affirmation also "contains nothing positive: no content can bind it [...]. Perhaps it is simply an affirmation of division."[34] Concluding, Foucault asserts that "[n]othing is more alien to this experience than the demonic character who "[...] denies everything".

> Transgression opens up onto a scintillating and constantly affirmed world, a world without shadow or twilight, without that serpentine "no" that bites into fruits and lodges their contradictions at their core.[35]

2.1.3 Transgression in Christian tradition

According to Bataille, the complementary character of taboo and transgression is spoiled by the introduction of the Christian concept of original sin. For him, "Christianity is [...] a condition of servitude. With it begins the possibility of class society and the alienation of the individual from society"[36]. It could prove useful to take a short look at the complication that arises from Christian tradition, a blockade of the free interplay of taboo and transgression, when analysing a play from a period as 'religiously determined' as the beginning 17th century supposedly was.

In Manichean thought, for which Bataille had particular interest, "guilt was inherent in the condition of being alive [...], had nothing to do with our own personal being" and thus left "[...] no possibility of salvation". Christianity, on the contrary, by virtue of having transformed the elemental, objectless sense of guilt "into a fault that inheres mankind", brings with it the need "[...] to give it an object and thus the notion of original sin arises". While "[...] it was Christianity that introduced the idea of original sin, we can also see in Christianity a will to deny the reality of sin (as it is tied to transgression) and the sense of a collective guilt with which it is associated."[37] Therefore, the "[...] urge of Christianity is towards a guilt-free condition." In this will to escape from

---

[33] Faubion, James, Ed. Aesthetics, Method, and Epistemology: Essential Works of Foucault p. 74
[34] Faubion, James, Ed. Aesthetics, Method, and Epistemology: Essential Works of Foucault p. 74
[35] Faubion, James, Ed. Aesthetics, Method, and Epistemology: Essential Works of Foucault p. 75
[36] Richardson, Michael. Georges Bataille p. 105
[37] Richardson, Michael. Georges Bataille p. 105

guilt, Bataille sees "the sickness brought to the world by Christianity"[38]. The notion of original sin is accompanied by the possibility of salvation:

> If we are shown to be at fault, then we can rectify our crime and regain our primal innocence. We can achieve this only through strict adherence with the taboo, which in the process is legitimated against transgressive behaviour (rather than being complementary to it). Instead of guilt, it is now the abstract notion of the law that becomes the condition of human society and transgression, the witness of man's guilt, is expelled.[39]

Thus Christianity broke the "relative harmony"[40] of the primitive state. Christianity bears an impulse "[...] to destroy social bonds by asserting that the only bond is between man and the god who is presented as his creator"[41]. Therefore, Christians define themselves not in relation to reality, but through their relation to "something that is beyond the world"[42]. "This further reinforces the extent to which the taboo is affirmed at the expense of the transgression"[43].

2.2 Discussion of *A Revenger's Tragedy*

2.2.1 Vindice as a revenger – a virtuous villain?

The character of Vindice, we already noted that, is an ambiguous one. He commits acts of great cruelty, but seems to have some form of "moral credit": he has been wronged beforehand. His betrothed Gloriana had been raped by the duke and, out of grief, poisoned herself. There is also an unfollowed hint that Vindice's father came to death "of discontent, the nobleman's consumption"[44]. Corresponding to the shifting speed of the play (scenes of vigorous action and multiple killing alternate with scenes of melancholy brooding) Vindice is subject to an "[...] alternation of pace and mood [...], now the witty deviser of schemes, now the anguished and melancholy mourner [...]"[45]. Concerning his problematic moral standing, it will be useful to take a look at the genre of revenge tragedy in general:

---

[38] Richardson, Michael. Georges Bataille p. 105
[39] Richardson, Michael. Georges Bataille p. 106
[40] Richardson, Michael. Georges Bataille p. 107
[41] Richardson, Michael. Georges Bataille p. 107
[42] Richardson, Michael. Georges Bataille p. 107
[43] Richardson, Michael. Georges Bataille p. 107
[44] Tourneur, Cyril. The Revenger's Tragedy (I. i, 125f) p. 9
[45] Tourneur, Cyril. The Revenger's Tragedy xvi

In one sense, the protagonist of the revenge plot becomes a complex character purely by virtue of his position in the web of intrigue that surrounds him. Drawn into his role by another's crime, [the revenger] is never a simple villain, for he does not initiate the events that lead to the acts of violence he eventually performs. However much he becomes enmired in evil, he has at some point in the play aroused a sense of engagement in spectators who pity his misfortunes and sympathize with his feelings of helplessness.[46]

This is exactly the case with Vindice. He starts off as a victim and gradually becomes more and more villain, plotting against his enemies. What Rozett says specifically of Hamlet is also true for him: he plays "[…] the role of one who is passing through what is both an ordeal or infliction, and a triumph" - he frequently gloats over his own wittiness, takes on himself the 'ordeal' of purging the court and in the very end, nearly stoically, accepts the sentence of death.

What concerns the intended response of the contemporary audience, we can assume, that "[…] on the matter of revenge the Elizabethans were caught between conflicting ethical systems. Despite the biblical injunction to leave revenge to God, there had been a long tradition of private revenge in England" (given that Elizabethan audiences did not distinctly differ from Jacobean in this aspect). So the ambiguities of our protagonist were obviously originally intended. We could trace them back to Aristotle's invocation of "pity and fear" which, according to his *Poetics,* should be the aim of every tragedy[47]. One of the play's main concerns and its distinctive, peculiar feature thereby is "the presentation of a deeply ironic and disquieting view of human nature"[48].

2.2.2 Vindice, Piato and the 'entirely other'

'Disquieting' is a great description indeed when it comes to the subject of our discussion. It perfectly describes our normal reaction to the piercing bullets of the heterogeneous. We have to face it in the mortality of our bodies, in putrefaction, corpses, excrement, arbitrariness, absolute power and chaos. All these things represent the fissure within ourselves, the recognition of which inspires us with such fear that we, unable to suppress these occurrences, constantly try to seal them into homogeneous shells – the classic function of ritual and religion[49]. Such shells serve to make our lives bear-

---

[46] Rozett, Martha. The Doctrine of Election and the Emergence of Elizabethan Tragedy. p. 174
[47] cp. Rozett, Martha. The Doctrine of Election and the Emergence of Elizabethan Tragedy. p. 178
[48] Tourneur, Cyril. The Revenger's Tragedy xvi
[49] in our days, as a surrogate to religion, these function is to great extent fulfilled by consumerism and science;

able, to decorate 'the horror'[50]; at the same time they are deceptive. This usually disguised 'other' blinks to us from *A Revenger's Tragedy* in various forms. There are several 'disquieting' instances were the orderly picture of the world is under threat, were there is no room left for re-establishing homogeneity – let us examine how Vindice copes with this and where his strategy is presented to lead him.

In the probably most famous revenge tragedy of all, Shakespeare's *Hamlet*, a ghost serves as the "catalyst triggering the protagonist's transformation"[51] to a villain – Gloriana's skull in *A Revenger's Tragedy*, 'death's vizard'[52], serves similar ends. When Vindice bitterly meditates on his lost love in the beginning, this skull becomes a symbol of the forces that "[plunge] the revenger into madness and gradually [transform] him from a good and respected man into an 'other'"[53].

What this 'other' means to us will gradually become clear if we take the detour of a 'receptive' interpretation of Vindice's part.

If we assume that he is a 'virtuous' person in the beginning, a typical, yet aristocrat subject, there is only one difference that distinguishes him from the people in the audience: for him, time has come to fight what he cannot bear any longer. Two questions immediately arise:

[1.] What does he fight against?

In the first place, of course, he fights the duke. He fights the person who has wronged him. But let's suppose for a moment it would not have been the duke who had been responsible for his lady's and father's death (actually, the responsibilities here are not that definite anyway), let's suppose it would have been an earthquake. Or a flood, plane crash or asteroid – Vindice, then, would have to fight – whom? Nature, fate itself because it is 'unfair', odd and incomprehensible, making us subject to forces outside the homogeneous. Vindice's (inner) torment, then, becomes universal – we all can recognize our own struggles in his, we all have the wish to find someone to hold responsible for the brutalities of life. He becomes a person of identification and that grants him our initial sympathy. The duke, from this point of view, becomes a convenient projection pane, mortal and punishable in contrary to fate. Vindice can kill him. Vindice kills him.

---

[50] in the referred edition of *A Revenger's Tragedy* there is a fitting illustration of a „Richly robed death grinning beneath a mask of youthful life" – Jacobeans, it seems, with their constantly recurring theme of 'memento mori', where much more aware of the madness of their world than we are today (Tourneur, Cyril. A Revenger's Tragedy p. xiv)

[51] Rozett, Martha. The Doctrine of Election and the Emergence of Elizabethan Tragedy. p. 182

[52] Tourneur, Cyril. A Revenger's Tragedy p. 6

[53] Rozett, Martha. The Doctrine of Election and the Emergence of Elizabethan Tragedy. p. 182

But [2.] if the duke thus really represents an instance of heterogeneity, how does Vindice achieve his aim? The devices he uses to fight this 'other' (in concrete terms, a person who has executive power, i.e. an intermediary to the realm of heterogeneity - the duke is thus doubly marked as heterogeneous) are necessarily little different from the duke's own devices. Vindice steps out of the homogeneous frame, and he does so by transgression. But different from what Bataille's transgression implied, a completion of the taboo, we can see Vindice, in transgressing, becoming 'other' himself.

The apparent transformation Vindice undergoes (from subject to revenger, simultaneously from 'righteous' to 'villain') is emphasized by his imaginary transformation[54] to Piato. Furthermore, this transformation occurs within an atmosphere of inverted values[55], presenting the whole world as already 'turned upside-down':

> The worlds so chang'd one shape into another,
> It is a wise child now that knows her mother.[56]

Or:

> Is the day out o'the socket,
> That it is noon at midnight [...]?[57]

To point out the connection of Vindice's transformation to that of the world, Hippolito recommends 'Piato' for the duke's office by the words:

> This our age swims within him; and if Time
> Had so much hair I should take him for Time,
> He is so near kin to this present minute.[58]

The image of Vindice's 'crossing the line' is sketched in the first scene when he holds Gloriana's skull, remnant of a dead body and subject to a taboo of physical contact. A first hint of transgression.

The last brush-stroke on this image will be when Vindice-Piato uses this tabooed skull as murder weapon towards the duke, who kisses it – and dies. Vindice, at that point, has violated a whole bundle of first-rate taboos: he kills his authority and uses the poisoned parts of a corpse to do it (later – Act V, scene i - he will even prop up the duke's corpse to 'have it murdered once more'). This adding-up of transgressive elements sounds quite absurd and gives a profound comical element to the play. But beneath all comical, we see transgression itself somehow getting a negative label attached to it. Vindice's worm-hole to the heterogeneous is presented to have the effect of a drug – the audience

---

[54]cf. Murray, Peter B. The Revenger's Tragedy and Transformation p. 68
[55] cf. Murray, Peter B. The Revenger's Tragedy and Transformation p. 65
[56] Tourneur, Cyril. The Revenger's Tragedy (II. iii, 45f) p. 47
[57] Tourneur, Cyril. The Revenger's Tragedy (I, iii, 45f) p. 47
[58] Tourneur, Cyril. The Revenger's Tragedy (I, iii, 24ff) p. 18

sees him getting addicted to cruelty and sucked more and more into it. It is a sadist we must see in him (and it may satisfy sadistic fantasies), when Vindice addresses the already dying duke:

> What, is thy tongue not eaten out yet?
> Then we'll invent a silence.
> [...]
> Nail down his tongue [...]; if he but gasp, he dies [...].
> If he but wink, [...]
> Let our two other hands tear up his lids
> And make his eyes, like comets, shine through blood.
> When he bleeds, then is the tragedy good.[59]

Here, at the latest, we, as audience, must begin to feel uneasy about Vindice's actions (and about our sympathies), the scales tip against him.

Eventually, however ambiguous the moral issues may have been during the earlier parts of the play, we are not left alone with judging Vindice: after the massacre-like finale, Antonio, who plays a very marginal role up to that point (he is the friend of Vindice's brother and also a victim of the duke's lechery), re-establishes order and helps realizing the 'evil nature' of Vindice's deeds. He gives a sense that the nightmare – and the topsy-turvidom - is over.

Vindice's transgression, then, turns out to be beneficial, to have purged the duke's devilish court. Murray suggests that the underlying principle is "a demonic, ironic justice, oblivious of good and evil, but working to destroy evil-doers"[60]. Transgression enables, with Antonio, a renewed start into homogeneity. The beginning of Antonio's reign as a duke marks the step back across the line and the closure of its horizon – but his first official act is the execution of the two persons who have 'borrowed' the power of the heterogeneous:

> My good! Away with 'em! Such an old man as he!
> You that would murder him would murder me![61]

At the outset, we saw Vindice as the incarnation of the anguished cry of man in the iron clasp of the heterogeneous - a cry that reverberated all through the audience. He became the hero for the terrified mortal who wouldn't himself dare to pursue the only way that promised alleviation: a complicity with what he fears most and yet is attracted to – the 'entirely other' or 'heterogeneous'; being so consequent, Vindice had to become a demi-god, take fate in his own hands. But now we see this universal fantasy counter-

---

[59] Tourneur, Cyril. The Revenger's Tragedy (III. v, 188-198) p. 64
[60] Murray, Peter B. The Revenger's Tragedy and Transformation p. 66
[61] Tourneur, Cyril. The Revenger's Tragedy (V. iii, 104ff) p. 107

pointed in the end by the revelation of (what is presented to us as) its hubris – a transformed Vindice, Tourneur shows us, is now himself so rotten that he is even unable to hold back his pride and must reveal his schemes to Antonio:

> We may be bold
> To speak it now: 'twas somewhat wittily carried
> Though we say it. 'Twas we who murdered him![62]

Murray observes that "[a]t the end of the play, [...] the author makes us see that the drive of Vindice and Hippolito to transform an evil court into a good one by violence ends in the same way as the drive of Supervacuo and Ambitioso to overthrow the state and obtain power for themselves." Like Supervacuo and Ambitioso, Vindice and his party mask themselves to get rid of Lussurioso. Vindice and Hippolito thus become even "physically indistinguishable from Supervacuo and Ambitioso"[63].

Rozett gives us a general reason for the revenger's damnation:

> Predictably, what damns the revenger is his presumption; he takes God's role upon himself, employing the concealed strategems, the sudden unveiling of purpose behind events, the patient biding of time, and the well-chosen punishments that typify God's control of human events[64].

What Rozett calls God here[65] appears to us as the heterogeneous element in our lives (so that the word 'control' collapses instantly) that Vindice dared to challenge and seize; he fought fire with fire - and Tourneur suggests that he has eventually been 'burnt by his own flame' - that the overturned, inverted world has, through Vindice, finally 'consumed itself':

> [...] Bear up
> Those tragic bodies; 'tis a heavy season
> Pray heaven their blood may wash away all treason.[66]

3. Conclusion

So, the play's attitude towards Vindice's behaviour – towards transgression - remains ambiguous. Vindice certainly fulfils audiences' fantasies, his amok even has a certain beneficent effect on society; but nevertheless it is presented as wrong. Vindice

---

[62] Tourneur, Cyril. The Revenger's Tragedy (V, iii, 96ff) p. 106

[63] Murray, Peter B. The Revenger's Tragedy and Transformation p. 72

[64] Rozett, Martha. The Doctrine of Election and the Emergence of Elizabethan Tragedy. p. 180

[65] withinin our theoretical frame certainly the masterpiece of homogenization, "the word that surpasses all other words" – concealing heterogeneity itself in the shell of "God's ways are inscrutable")

[66] Tourneur, Cyril. The Revenger's Tragedy (V, iii, 128) p. 108

is not allowed to come back to the cradle of homogeneity. He remains a madman, in the end, and cannot be redeemed. It seems that Tourneur wasn't fully convinced of what Foucault and Bataille said about transgression, that it wouldn't spoil the taboo. The world of *A Revenger's Tragedy* is just not the same as the world of Foucault's transgression, this world without twilight and shadow which is constantly affirmed - rather the contrary. It is here that we have to take into account the complications of Christianity Bataille mentioned, it is exactly this 'affirmation of the taboo at the expense of transgression' that we can observe in Tourneur's didactic effort; although we have to note that the world of *A Revenger's Tragedy* is a world in a particularly fallen state, perhaps more in Manichean than in Christian tradition – while 'speedy damnation' lingers everywhere[67], salvation and repentance are virtually non-existent (when the duke begs for "months [...] with penitential heaves"[68], it is only a device for being spared from murder). Accordingly, the agent of transgression in Tourneur doesn't come back behind the line anymore, he is not at all the same when the 'orgy' is over; he rather constitutes an imbalance then, and it looks as if therefore he receives a label of 'low heterogeneity' - of a threat that must immediately be sealed away. Accordingly, to reestablish the static equilibrium of society, he is expelled (as alternatives to killing him, they could have put him into jail or the lunatic asylum; the effect would be the same). Taking now into account the polarized character of the heterogeneous realm, we can say that the 'imperial heterogeneous', personified in Antonio, takes care of the excretion of the 'low heterogeneous' element Vindice to fulfil its function of safeguarding the static equilibrium.

This, Tourneur seems to say to the audience, this is what life has in store for those who act that way. Vindice's expulsion is presented as the inevitable outcome of transgression. And by his final bowing to this inevitable, Vindice regains some of the audience's sympathies by 'seeing his mistake'. From that point of view, he takes the duke, his family and a corrupted court with him down the drain. Tourneur implies in a certain sense that it is 'useless to revolt'. The audiences are being affirmed that, however promising, it would be wrong to resist.

Had Tourneur given us a happy ending, it would have given a completely different moral twist to the play. Such an ending – with Vindice as the new duke - would really have given a subversive element to it; it would have given audiences the idea of 'destroying what destroys you can improve your situation', or 'resistance is not futile'.

---

[67] cf. Tourneur, Cyril. The Revenger's Tragedy (II, ii, 10) p. 45
[68] Tourneur, Cyril. The Revenger's Tragedy (II, ii, 10) p. 45

However, to avoid the semblance that Vindice is a genuine revolutionary, we have to note that he doesn't at any point aim to overturn the state or the fabric of society in a 'revolutionary' sense. Although, by virtue of its universal character, as we have shown, his outrage is more than a private vendetta, it remains less than an actual coup d'état. Therefore, *A Revenger's Tragedy* is as far as it could be from being a subversive play.

It might nevertheless be interesting, with respect to Tourneur's didactic effort, to note a conspicuous parallel to two famous and really subversive murderers: the best-known tyrannicides of all history, Cassius and Brutus, who, in the end (due to the fervent speech of yet another Antonius, by the way) failed, in spite of killing Caesar, and were, much like Vindice, equipped with the label 'threat to society' – they were not only put to death, but even went straight into the ninth circle of hell. As story[69] has it, they joined Judas Iscariot there, and the Prince of Darkness himself is eternally gnawing on the three 'ultimate sinners' heads.

---

[69] according to Dante Alighieri's *Divina Commedia;*

4. Works Cited

Bataille, Georges. *Der heilige Eros*. Trans. Max Hölzer.
Frankfurt a. M.: Ullstein, 1982

Gasché, Rodolphe. The Heterological Almanac. Leslie Anne Boldt-Irons, Ed. a.
Trans. *On Bataille: Critical Essays*.
New York: New York UP, 1995

Faubion, James, Ed. *Aesthetics, Method, and Epistemology: Essential Works of
Foucault, Volume 2*. Trans. Robert Hurley et al. 2nd ed. London: Penguin, 1998

Seitter, Walter, Ed. a. Trans. *Von der Subversion des Wissens*. München: Hanser,
1974

Murray, Peter B. The Revenger's Tragedy and Transformation. R. V. Holdsworth,
Ed. *Three Jacobean Revenge Tragedies: A Casebook*. London:
Macmillan, 1990

Richardson, Michael. *Georges Bataille*. London: Routledge, 1994

Rozett, Martha. *The Doctrine of Election and the Emergence of Elizabethan
Tragedy*. Princeton, New Jersey: Princeton UP, 1984

Tourneur, Cyril. *The Revenger's Tragedy*. Ed. Brain Gibbons. 6th ed.
London: A & C Black, 1987

Wiechens, Peter. *Bataille zur Einführung*. Hamburg: Junius, 1995

Lightning Source UK Ltd.
Milton Keynes UK
233262UK00001B/7